DEC 2018

D0004527

Where in the World Can I . . .

HIKE A CANYON?

Where in the World Can I . . .

HIKE A CANYON?

WORLD
BOOK

www.worldbook.com

World Book, Inc.
180 North LaSalle Street, Suite 900
Chicago, Illinois 60601
USA

For information about other World Book
publications, visit our website at
www.worldbook.com or call
1-800-WORLDBK (967-5325).

For information about sales to schools and
libraries, call 1-800-975-3250 (United States),
or 1-800-837-5365 (Canada).

Library of Congress Cataloging-in-Publication
Data for this volume has been applied for.

Where in the World Can I…
ISBN: 978-0-7166-2178-2 (set, hc.)

Hike a Canyon?
ISBN: 978-0-7166-2183-6 (hc.)

Also available as:
ISBN: 978-0-7166-2193-5 (e-book)

Printed in China by Shenzhen Wing King Tong
Paper Products Co., Ltd., Shenzhen, Guangdong
1st printing July 2018

STAFF

Writer: Shawn Brennan

Executive Committee
President
Jim O'Rourke

Vice President and
Editor in Chief
Paul A. Kobasa

Vice President, Finance
Donald D. Keller

Vice President, Marketing
Jean Lin

Vice President,
International Sales
Maksim Rutenberg

Vice President, Technology
Jason Dole

Director, Human Resources
Bev Ecker

Editorial
Director, New Print
Tom Evans

Managing Editor, New Print
Jeff De La Rosa

Senior Editor, New Print
Shawn Brennan

Editor, New Print
Grace Guibert

Librarian
S. Thomas Richardson

Manager, Contracts &
Compliance (Rights &
Permissions)
Loranne K. Shields

Manager, Indexing Services
David Pofelski

Digital
Director, Digital Product
Development
Erika Meller

Manager, Digital Products
Jonathan Wills

Graphics and Design
Senior Art Director
Tom Evans

Coordinator, Design
Development and
Production
Brenda Tropinski

Media Researcher
Rosalia Bledsoe

**Manufacturing/
Production**
Manufacturing Manager
Anne Fritzinger

Proofreader
Nathalie Strassheim

TABLE OF CONTENTS

WHAT IS A CANYON?

A canyon is a deep valley with steep sides. Most canyons have been made by rivers or streams. The flow of the water slowly wears away rock. Canyons cut by rivers or streams typically have a V shape.

In mountain areas, canyons are sometimes made by *glaciers (GLAY shuhrz).* A glacier is a large, thick sheet of ice that moves slowly over the land. Canyons made by glaciers usually have a *U* shape.

A narrow canyon with walls or cliffs that are nearly straight up and down is called a *gorge (gawrj)*, *ravine (ruh VEEN)*, or *chasm (KAZ uhm)*.

Long, narrow bays called *fiords (fyohrdz)* have steep, rocky walls with thick woods and tumbling waterfalls. (A *bay* is an area of ocean or lake water that has pushed into the land.) Fiords formed on coastlines where the sea level rose and flooded canyons. Rivers may have cut these canyons millions of years ago. Then glaciers made them even deeper.

Faulting is the movement of the huge areas that make up Earth's top layer, or crust. Faulting has created many of the large canyons on the ocean floor.

Earth is not the only planet in our solar system that has canyons. The planet Mars has a huge chain of canyons. The canyon chain is about 2,500 miles (4,000 kilometers) long and 5 to 6 miles (8 to 10 kilometers) deep in some places. The chain of canyons is long enough to stretch across the entire width of Australia!

YOU MIGHT THINK YOU ARE ON ANOTHER PLANET WHEN YOU VISIT SOME OF EARTH'S SPECTACULAR CANYONS! LET'S HIKE THROUGH A FEW.

THE GRAND CANYON

The Grand Canyon is one of the largest, most beautiful, and most famous canyons in the world. It cuts through northwestern Arizona in Grand Canyon National Park in the southwestern United States. The canyon is about 1 mile (1.6 kilometers) deep. It is 277 miles (446 kilometers) long. The width of the canyon varies. In some places it is less than 1 mile (1.6 kilometers) wide, and in other places it is 18 miles (29 kilometers) wide.

This is what the Grand Canyon looks like from space!

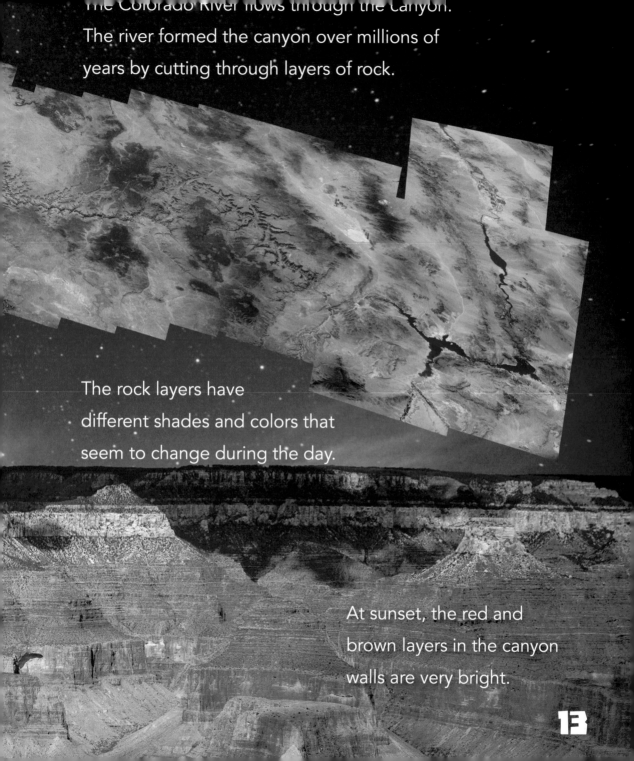

The Colorado River flows through the canyon. The river formed the canyon over millions of years by cutting through layers of rock.

The rock layers have different shades and colors that seem to change during the day.

At sunset, the red and brown layers in the canyon walls are very bright.

13

The Grand Canyon has several different kinds of climate. *Climate* is the kind of weather a place usually gets. The climate at the bottom of the canyon is much warmer and drier than the climate at the top. Because of these differences in climate, a wide variety of plants and animals live in the canyon.

There are many tall ponderosa
(PON duh ROH suh) pine trees on
the canyon's rim, or top edge. On the south
side of the canyon, juniper *(JOO nuh puhr)* and
piñon *(PIHN yuhn* or *PEEN yohn)* pines grow in the
lower areas. Aspen, fir, and spruce trees are found in
the highest areas on the north side. Cactuses grow
throughout the canyon, especially in the low areas.

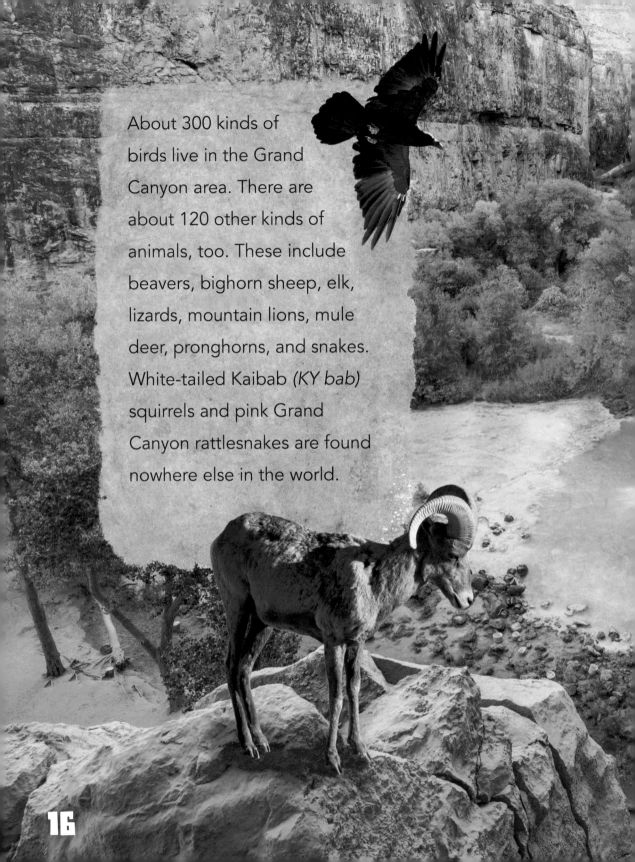

About 300 kinds of birds live in the Grand Canyon area. There are about 120 other kinds of animals, too. These include beavers, bighorn sheep, elk, lizards, mountain lions, mule deer, pronghorns, and snakes. White-tailed Kaibab *(KY bab)* squirrels and pink Grand Canyon rattlesnakes are found nowhere else in the world.

Different American Indian groups have lived in the Grand Canyon over the last 4,000 years. Today, about 300 Havasupai (*HAH vuh SOO py*) Indians live in a side canyon called Havasu (*HAH vuh SOO*) Canyon.

Havasupai means *people of the blue-green water.*

The deepest part of the Grand Canyon has rocks that date back 2 billion years. The Colorado River began to form the Grand Canyon about 6 million years ago. Over time, the water wore away the layers of rock, forming the canyon. Fossils found in the canyon walls show that animals and plants lived in the area millions of years ago. A *fossil* is the remains of a living thing that died long ago.

brachiopod

fern

trilobite

In 1540, some Spanish explorers became the first Europeans to see the Grand Canyon. The American *geologist* (scientist who studies rocks) John Wesley Powell explored the Grand Canyon in 1869 and gave the canyon its name. The Grand Canyon has been called one of the seven natural wonders of the world. This is an unofficial list of spectacular natural objects on Earth.

JOHN WESLEY POWELL

1869 EXPEDITION

6¢ U.S. POSTAGE

GRAND CANYON NATIONAL PARK

Grand Canyon National Park was established in 1919. It consists almost entirely of the Grand Canyon. It is one of the most popular national parks in the United States. The park also includes steep hills, tall spires of rock, and other amazing landforms.

Most visitors drive along park roads and stop at scenic viewing points along the Grand Canyon. Visitors may also walk along the canyon's rim. Many tourists hike trails in the park. Some people ride mules into the canyon. Others enter by boat or raft on the Colorado River.

The South Rim of the Grand Canyon is the most developed part of Grand Canyon National Park. Most of the visitors view the canyon from this area. The headquarters of the park are at Grand Canyon Village, on the South Rim of the canyon. Major viewing points along the South Rim include Desert View, Mather Point, and Hermit's Rest. The South Rim is open to visitors throughout the year.

The North Rim begins about 10 miles (16 kilometers) away on the other side of the canyon. Visitors may drive around the canyon or hike across the bottom from one side to the other. The distance around the canyon to the North Rim by road is 220 miles (354 kilometers). The hiking distance by trail across the canyon is almost 21 miles (34 kilometers). The trail takes most visitors at least two days to hike. Major viewing points on the North Rim are Bright Angel Point, Cape Royal, and Point Imperial. The North Rim is closed from late October to mid-May because of heavy snow.

Grand Canyon National Park has dozens of hiking trails, covering hundreds of miles or kilometers. The three main trails into the canyon are Bright Angel and South Kaibab, which begin on the South Rim, and North Kaibab, starting on the North Rim. These trails connect on the bottom of the canyon at Phantom Ranch. The ranch has cabins, a dining hall, and a campground. Visitors may make reservations to stay at Phantom Ranch.

Half-day and one-day trips by mule into the Grand Canyon begin on both the North and South rims. Two-day trips begin only on the South Rim. Visitors who take the two-day trip spend the night at Phantom Ranch.

Visitors may travel by boat or raft down the Colorado River as it flows east to west through the Grand Canyon. Private companies provide most of the river trips, but visitors with the proper skill and equipment may get permits to travel the river on their own.

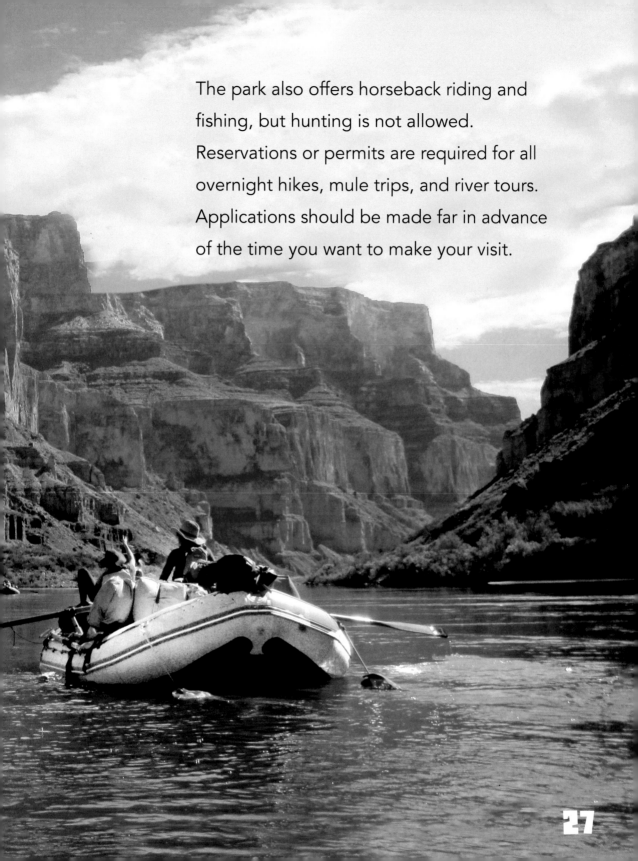

The park also offers horseback riding and fishing, but hunting is not allowed. Reservations or permits are required for all overnight hikes, mule trips, and river tours. Applications should be made far in advance of the time you want to make your visit.

Changes in the environment are harming Grand Canyon National Park. Air pollution that blows in from Los Angeles, California, often makes it hard to see the canyon's views. The city is about 300 miles (480 kilometers) from the park. Also, the park's environment has suffered from the building of dams upstream on the Colorado River.

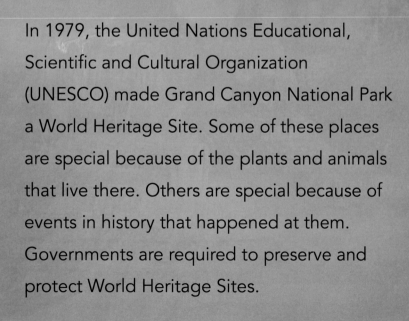

Changes in the flow of water change the ecosystem. This harms water birds and other wildlife in the park. (An *ecosystem* is made up of the living things in an area and the nonliving things they depend on.)

In 1979, the United Nations Educational, Scientific and Cultural Organization (UNESCO) made Grand Canyon National Park a World Heritage Site. Some of these places are special because of the plants and animals that live there. Others are special because of events in history that happened at them. Governments are required to preserve and protect World Heritage Sites.

OTHER AMAZING HIKES

MILFORD TRACK

How would you like to tramp the "finest walk in the world?" (In New Zealand, taking a long, vigorous walk or hike is called *tramping*.) That's what trampers have called Milford Track in New Zealand's Fiordland *(fyawrd land)* National Park. The track is on Milford Sound, a scenic sea outlet on the west coast of the South Island.

Fiordland is New Zealand's largest national park. It covers about 4,800 square miles (12,500 square kilometers) on the South Island. The park is named for its narrow fiords between high cliffs. These fiords are up to 27 miles (43 kilometers) long and about 1,600 feet (500 meters) deep.

The park also includes
evergreen rain forests and
Sutherland Falls, which
drops 1,904 feet (580
meters). You'll tramp along
these rain forests, fiords,
waterfalls, and mountains
on Milford Track's 33-mile
(53.5-kilometer) route.
Mackinnon Pass is the
track's highest point. It is
3,787 feet (1,154 meters)
above sea level. Some
14,000 people tramp the
track each year.

You will also be tramping through history on Milford Track. New Zealand's native Māori (*MOW ree* or *MAH ree*) people used the track for gathering and transporting valuable greenstone, a form of jade. You may also trace the footsteps of early New Zealand explorers. They include Scottish explorers Donald Sutherland, who discovered what now is called Sutherland Falls in 1880, and Quintin Mackinnon, who discovered today's Mackinnon Pass in 1888.

In 1986, UNESCO added Fiordland National Park to its World Heritage List. The park is listed as part of the Te Wāhipounamu (*teh WAH hee POH nuh moo*) World Heritage Area.

WADI RUM

How about a hike on the moon? You might feel like you are hiking on the moon if you travel to Wadi Rum *(WAH dee RUHM)*, a desert valley in southern Jordan. Jordan is an Arab kingdom east of the Jordan River in the Middle East. A *wadi* is a usually dry valley or ravine. A stream flows through a wadi in the rainy season. Wadi Rum has a spectacular landscape of arches, canyons, cliffs, mountains, pink sands, and rocky desert. Because of its unearthly appearance, Wadi Rum is sometimes called the "Valley of the Moon."

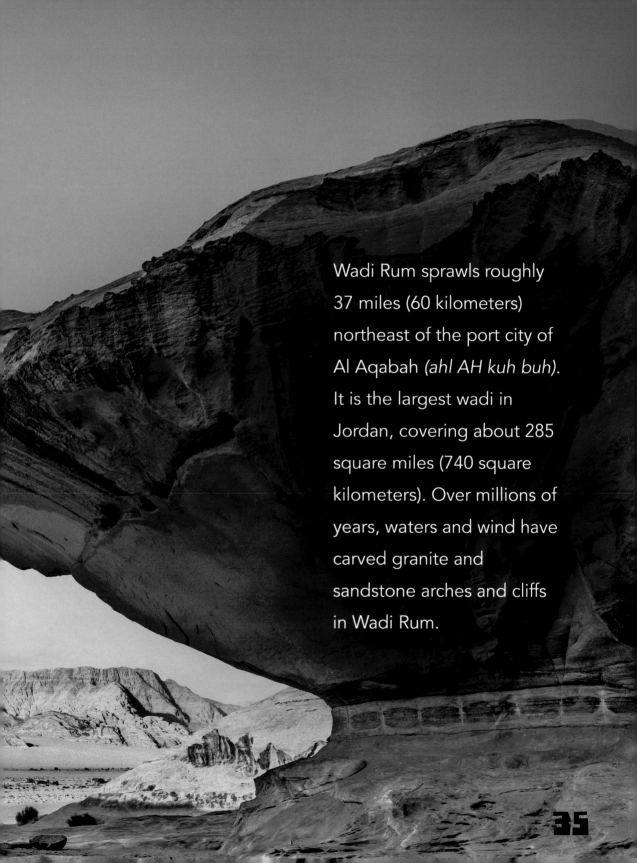

Wadi Rum sprawls roughly 37 miles (60 kilometers) northeast of the port city of Al Aqabah *(ahl AH kuh buh)*. It is the largest wadi in Jordan, covering about 285 square miles (740 square kilometers). Over millions of years, waters and wind have carved granite and sandstone arches and cliffs in Wadi Rum.

The wadi's many mountains
include Jordan's second highest
peak, Jabal Ramm *(JAH bahl
RAHM)*. It rises 5,755 feet (1,754
meters) above sea level. Only
nearby Jabal Umm ad Dami *(JAH
bahl oom ahd DAH mee)* is taller.
It rises 6,083 feet (1,854 meters)
above sea level.

Rainstorms sometimes cause flash floods in Wadi Rum during winter. A *flash flood* is a sudden rush of water on dry land. Snow may fall in the mountain peaks. Nighttime temperatures often fall below freezing. In summer, daytime temperatures can soar above 105 °F (40 °C).

A few springs have created small *oases (oh AY seez)* within Wadi Rum. An *oasis (oh AY sis)* is an area in the desert where underground water is close to the surface. (*Oases* is the plural of *oasis*.)

Some acacia *(uh KAY shuh)* and fig trees grow in Wadi Rum's harsh landscape, along with bushy clumps of grass.

fennec

Beetles, scorpions, reptiles, small birds, and birds of prey live throughout wadi canyons. A *bird of prey* is a large bird that hunts and eats other animals. *Nocturnal* (night) mammals in the wadi include jerboas *(juhr BOH uhz)*, fennecs *(FEHN ehks)*, and caracals *(KAR uh kalz)*. A jerboa is a rodent that looks like a tiny kangaroo. A fennec is a small fox with huge ears. A caracal is a member of the cat family.

jerboa

caracal

People have lived in Wadi Rum for thousands of years. Ancient Arab peoples left behind thousands of writings and other rock carvings in the wadi. They also built temples there.

Today, Bedouin *(BEHD u ihn)* peoples live in Wadi Rum. Their tents and goat herds are seen across the area. Zalabia *(ZEHL uh BEE uh)* Bedouin live in Rum village, where they organize things for tourists. Zalabia guides lead campers, hikers, and rock climbers throughout the wadi.

During World War I (1914-1918), Arab armies in Wadi Rum revolted against Ottoman *(OT uh muhn)* rule. The Ottoman Empire was centered in what is now Turkey. The Ottomans had entered the war on the side of the Germans, against the British.

The British soldier and writer T. E. Lawrence played an important role in the revolt. In 1917, he and an Arab army captured Ottoman-held Aqabah. Lawrence also led raids on Ottoman posts and railways from Wadi Rum. He became known as Lawrence of Arabia.

Lawrence wrote about Wadi Rum in his book, *Seven Pillars of Wisdom* (1926). The book described his adventures in the Arabian Peninsula. A large mountain in Wadi Rum is named after Lawrence's book. Many spots in the area claim connections to events in Lawrence's life.

Jordan's government declared Wadi Rum a protected area in 1998. A visitors' complex was added in the early 2000's. The Wadi Rum Protected Area became a World Heritage Site in 2011.

HIKING SAFETY

Each year, many people get lost, injured, or even killed while hiking. Keep these tips in mind to make your hiking trip a safe and fun experience.

- Children should always hike with an adult.

- Do not hike alone if you are unfamiliar with a trail.

- Check weather forecasts before you hike.

- Before you hike, tell your destination and expected length of the hike to someone who will not be hiking.

- Call or visit the headquarters of the park or forest where you will be hiking before you hike. Ask about any special trail difficulties or hazards.

- Bring a trail map with you.

- Stay on marked trails and never leave the group.

- Wear lightweight clothing and sturdy hiking boots or shoes that fit you well.

- Drink plenty of water before and during the hike. Carry a water bottle and fill it at water stations.

- Carry lip balm, sunblock, insect repellent, and sunglasses—and use them!

- Carry emergency supplies, including a first-aid kit, extra food, matches, and a flashlight with batteries.

- If you get lost, keep calm, stay where you are, and wait for a search party to find you.

BOOKS AND WEBSITES

BOOKS

Extreme Planet: Carsten Peter's Adventures in Volcanoes, Caves, Canyons, Deserts, and Beyond! by Carsten Peter (National Geographic, 2015)
This illustrated book from National Geographic features exhilarating, first-hand accounts of visiting these natural wonders in some of the planet's most remote and inhospitable areas. Includes charts, graphs, maps, and hands-on activities and experiments.

Grand Canyon by Jason Chinn (Roaring Brook/Neal Porter, 2017)
This illustrated hiking tour features actual locations and views to take readers from the oldest, deepest area of the Grand Canyon (the Inner Gorge) to the youngest (Ponderosa Pine Forest).

Super Cool Science Experiments: Erosion by Ariel Kazunas and Charnan Simon (Cherry Lake, 2009)
This book offers a brief explanation of scientific examination, questioning, and hypothesis, as well as an overview of geology and erosion. Presents five experiments so children can examine the effects of chemical, biological, and mechanical weathering on various objects.

WEBSITES

Dynamic Earth
http://www.learner.org/interactives/dynamicearth/index.html

This interactive lesson teaches students about the structure and movement of Earth. At the end of the lesson, students can take a quiz to test their knowledge.

Rock Around The Park
http://www.webrangers.us/activities/rockpark/?id=22

Sponsored by the U.S. National Park Service, this site includes an interactive game that teaches kids about erosion and how it affects Earth's surface.

INDEX

ACKNOWLEDGMENTS

Cover: © Galyna Andrushko, Shutterstock

2-9 © Shutterstock

10-11 © Charles Hood, Alamy Images;
© Majivecka/Shutterstock

12-13 © Skreidzeleu/Shutterstock; NASA

14-15 © Shutterstock

16-17 © Shutterstock; © Bill Gozansky, Alamy Images

18-19 © Shutterstock

20-21 © Digital Vision/SuperStock

22-31 © Shutterstock

32-33 © Raclro/iStockphoto; © Jax10289/Shutterstock

34-35 © P Pictures/Shutterstock

36-37 © Liseykina/Dreamstime; © Menahem Kahana,
AFP/Getty Images

38-41 © Shutterstock

42-43 From *Lawrence of Arabia* (Columbia Pictures);
© Anton Ivanov, Shutterstock

44-45 © Shutterstock